Table of Contents

Taking Standardized Tests

No matter what grade you're in, this is information you can use to prepare for standardized tests. Here is what you'll find:

- Test-taking tips and strategies to use on test day and year-round.
- Important terms to know for Language Arts, Reading, Math, Science, and Social Studies.
- A checklist of skills to complete to help you understand what you need to know in Language Arts, Reading Comprehension, Writing, and Math.
- General study/homework tips.

By opening this book, you've already taken your first step towards test success. The rest is easy—all you have to do is get started!

What You Need to Know

There are many things you can do to increase your test success. Here's a list of tips to keep in mind when you take standardized tests—and when you study for them, too.

Keep up with your school work. One way you can succeed in school and on tests is by studying and doing your homework regularly. Studies show that you remember only about one-fifth of what you memorize the night before a test. That's one good reason not to try to learn it all at once! Keeping up with your work throughout the year will help you remember the material better. You also won't be as tired or nervous as if you try to learn everything at once.

Feel your best. One of the ways you can do your best on tests and in school is to make sure your body is ready. To do this, get a good night's sleep each night and eat a healthy breakfast (not sugary cereal that will leave you tired by the middle of the morning). An egg or a milkshake with yogurt and fresh fruit will give you lasting energy. Also, wear comfortable clothes, maybe your lucky shirt or your favorite color on test day. It can't hurt, and it may even keep you relax.

Be prepared. Do practice questions and learn about how standardized tests are organized. Books like this one will help you know what to expect when you take a standardized test.

When you are taking the test, follow the directions. It is important to listen carefully to the directions your teacher gives and to read the written instructions carefully. Words like *not*, *none*, *rarely*, *never*, and *always* are very important in test directions and questions. You may want to circle words like these.

Look at each page carefully before you start answering. In school you usually read a passage and then answer questions about it. But when you take a test, it's helpful to follow a different order.

If you are taking a Reading test, first read the directions. Then read the questions before you read the passage. This way you will know exactly what kind of information to look for as you read. Next, read the passage carefully. Finally, answer the questions.

On math and science tests, look at the labels on graphs and charts. Think about what each graph or chart shows. Questions often will ask you to draw conclusions about the information.

Manage your time. *Time management* means using your time wisely on a test so that you can finish as much of it as possible and do your best. Look over the test or the parts that you are allowed to do at one time. Sometimes you may want to do the easier parts first. This way, if you run out of time before you finish, you will have completed a good chunk of the work.

For tests that have a time limit, notice what time it is when the test begins and figure out when you need to stop. Check a few times as you work through the test to be sure you are making good progress and not spending too much time on any particular section.

You don't have to keep up with everyone else. You may notice other students in the class finishing before you do. Don't worry about this. Everyone works at a different pace. Just keep going, trying not to spend too long on any one question.

Fill in answer sheets properly. Even if you know every answer on a test, you won't do well unless you enter the answers correctly on the answer sheet.

Fill in the entire bubble, but don't spend too much time making it perfect. Make your mark dark, but not so dark that it goes through the paper! And be sure you only choose one answer for each question, even if you are not sure. If you choose two answers, both will be marked as wrong.

It's usually not a good idea to change your answers. Usually your first choice is the right one. Unless you realize that you misread the question, the directions, or some facts in a passage, it's usually safer to stay with your first answer. If you are pretty sure it's wrong, of course, go ahead and change it. Make sure you completely erase the first choice and neatly fill in your new choice.

Use context clues to figure out tough questions. If you come across a word or idea you don't understand, use context clues—the words in the sentences nearby—to help you figure out its meaning.

Sometimes it's good to guess. Should you guess when you don't know an answer on a test? That depends. If your teacher has made the test, usually you will score better if you answer as many questions as possible, even if you don't really know the answers.

On standardized tests, here's what to do to score your best. For each question, most of these tests let you choose from four or five answer choices. If you decide that a couple of answers are clearly wrong but you're still not sure about the answer, go ahead and make your best guess. If you can't narrow down the choices at all, then you may be better off skipping the question. Tests like these take away extra points for wrong answers, so it's better to leave them blank. Be sure you skip over the answer space for these questions on the answer sheet, though, so you don't fill in the wrong spaces.

Sometimes you should skip a question and come back to it later.

On many tests, you will score better if you answer more questions. This means that you should not spend too much time on any single question. Sometimes it gets tricky, though, keeping track of questions you skipped on your answer sheet.

If you want to skip a question because you don't know the answer, put a very light pencil mark next to the question in the test booklet. Try to choose an answer, even if you're not sure of it. Fill in the answer lightly on the answer sheet.

Check your work.
On a standardized test, you can't go ahead or skip back to another section of the test. But you may go back and review your answers on the section you just worked on if you have extra time.

First, scan your answer sheet. Make sure that you answered every question you could. Also, if you are using a bubble-type answer sheet, make sure that you filled in only one bubble for each question. Erase any extra marks on the page.

Finally—avoid test anxiety!
If you get nervous about tests, don't worry. *Test anxiety* happens to lots of good students. Being a little nervous actually sharpens your mind. But if you get very nervous about tests, take a few minutes to relax the night before or the day of the test. One good way to relax is to get some exercise, even if you just have time to stretch, shake out your fingers, and wiggle your toes. If you can't move around, it helps just to take a few slow, deep breaths and picture yourself doing a great job!

Terms to Know

Here's a list of terms that are good to know when taking standardized tests. Don't be worried if you see something new. You may not have learned it in school yet.

acute angle: an angle of less than 90°

adjective: a word that describes a noun (*yellow duckling*, *new bicycle*)

adverb: a word that describes a verb (*ran fast*, *laughing heartily*)

analogy: a comparison of the relationship between two or more otherwise unrelated things (*Carrot is to vegetable as banana is to fruit.*)

angle: the figure formed by two lines that start at the same point, usually shown in degrees **90°**

antonyms: words with opposite meanings (*big* and *small*, *young* and *old*)

area: the amount of space inside a flat shape, expressed in square units

article: a word such as *a*, *an*, or *the* that goes in front of a noun (*the chicken*, *an apple*)

cause/effect: the reason that something happens

character: a person in a story, book, movie, play, or TV show

compare/contrast: to tell what is alike and different about two or more things

compass rose: the symbol on a map that shows where North, South, East, and West are

conclusion: a logical decision you can make based on information from a reading selection or science experiment

congruent: equal in size or shape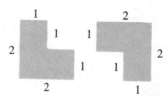

context clues: language and details in a piece of writing that can help you figure out difficult words and ideas

denominator: in a fraction, the number under the line; shows how many equal parts a whole has been divided into ($\frac{1}{2}$, $\frac{6}{7}$)

direct object: in a sentence, the person or thing that receives the action of a verb (*Jane hit the ball hard.*)

equation: in math, a statement where one set of numbers or values is equal to another set (*6 + 6 = 12, 4 x 5 = 20*)

factor: a whole number that can be divided exactly into another whole number (*1, 2, 3, 4, and 6 are all factors of 12.*)

genre: a category of literature that contains writing with common features (*drama, fiction, nonfiction, poetry*)

hypothesis: in science, the possible answer to a question; most science experiments begin with a hypothesis

indirect object: in a sentence, the noun or pronoun that tells to or for whom the action of the verb is done (*Louise gave a flower to her sister.*)

infer: to make an educated guess about a piece of writing, based on information contained in the selection and what you already know

main idea: the most important idea or message in a writing selection

map legend: the part of a map showing symbols that represent natural or human-made objects

noun: a person, place, or thing (*president, underground, train*)

numerator: in a fraction, the number above the line; shows how many equal parts are to be taken from the denominator ($\frac{3}{4}, \frac{1}{5}$)

operation: in math, tells what must be done to numbers in an equation (such as add, subtract, multiply, or divide)

parallel: lines or rays that, if extended, could never intersect

percent: fraction of a whole that has been divided into 100 parts, usually expressed with % sign ($\frac{5}{100} = 5\%$)

perimeter: distance around an object or shape

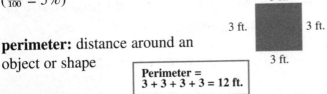

Perimeter =
3 + 3 + 3 + 3 = 12 ft.

perpendicular: lines or rays that intersect to form a 90° (right) angle

90°

predicate: in a sentence, the word or words that tell what the subject does, did, or has (*The fuzzy kitten had black spots on its belly.*)

predict: in science or reading, to use given information to decide what will happen

prefixes/suffixes: letters added to the beginning or end of a word to change its meaning (*reorganize, hopeless*)

preposition: a word that shows the relationship between a noun or pronoun and other words in a phrase or sentence (*We sat by the fire. She walked through the door.*)

probability: the likelihood that something will happen, often shown with numbers

pronoun: a word that is used in place of a noun (*She gave the present to them.*)

ratio: a comparison of two quantities, often shown as a fraction (*The ratio of boys to girls in the class is 2 to 1, or 2/1.*)

sequence: the order in which events happen or in which items can be placed in a pattern

subject: in a sentence, the word or words that tell who or what the sentence is about (*Uncle Robert baked the cake. Everyone at the party ate it.*)

summary: a restatement of important ideas from a selection in the writer's own words

symmetry: in math and science, two or more sides or faces of an object that are mirror images of one another

line of symmetry

synonyms: words with the same, or almost the same, meaning (*delicious* and *tasty, funny* and *comical*)

Venn diagram: two or more overlapping circles used to compare and contrast two or more things

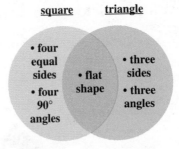

verb: a word that describes an action or state of being (*He watched the fireworks.*)

writing prompt: on a test, a question or statement that you must respond to in writing

Practice Test and
Final Test Information

The remainder of this book is made up of two tests. On page 16, you will find a Practice Test. On page 54, you will find a Final Test. These tests will give you a chance to put the tips you have learned to work.

Here are some things to remember as you take these tests:

• Be sure you understand all the directions before you begin each test.

• Ask an adult questions about the directions if you do not understand them.

• Work as quickly as you can during each test. There are no time limits on the Practice Test, but you should try to make good use of your time. There are suggested time limits on the Final Test to give you practice managing your time.

• You will notice little GO and STOP signs at the bottom of the test pages. When you see a GO sign, continue on to the next page if you feel ready. The STOP sign means you are at the end of a section. When you see a STOP sign, take a break.

• When you change an answer, be sure to erase your first mark completely.

• You can guess at an answer or skip difficult items and go back to them later.

• Use the tips you have learned whenever you can.

• After you have completed your tests, check your answers with the answer key.

• It is OK to be a little nervous. You may even do better.

• When you complete all the lessons in this book, you will be on your way to test success!

Multiple Choice Questions

You have probably seen multiple choice questions before. They are the most common type of question used on standardized tests. To answer a multiple choice question, you must choose one answer from a number of choices.

> **EXAMPLE** **The word that means the opposite of rapid is _____ .**
>
> Ⓐ shallow   Ⓒ speedy
>
> Ⓑ sluggish   Ⓓ rabbit

Sometimes you will know the answer right away. Other times you won't. To answer multiple choice questions on a test, do the following:

- Read the directions carefully. If you're not sure what you're supposed to do, you may make a lot of mistakes.
- First answer any easy questions whose answers you are *sure* you know.
- When you come to a harder question, circle the question number. You can come back to this question after you have finished all the easier ones.
- When you're ready to answer a hard question, throw out answers that you know are wrong. You can do this by making an **X** after each choice you know is not correct. The last choice left is probably the correct one.

Testing It Out

Now look at the sample question more closely.

Think: I know that rapid means "fast." So I must be looking for a word that means "slow." I have already eliminated *speedy* and *rabbit*. *Speedy* has the same meaning as *rapid*. *Rabbit* doesn't really have anything to do with *rapid*.

Now I have to choose between *shallow* and *sluggish*. *Shallow* means the opposite of *deep*, not the opposite of *fast*. I do not know the word *sluggish*, but I do know that slugs are slow-moving creatures. So I will choose **B**.

Fill-in-the-Blank Questions

On some tests, you will be given multiple choice questions where you must fill in something that's missing from a phrase, sentence, equation, or passage. These are called "fill-in-the-blank" questions.

EXAMPLE   **Pablo was looking _____ to his family's camping trip.**

Ⓐ foremost   Ⓒ former

Ⓑ forehead   Ⓓ forward

To answer fill-in-the-blank questions, do the following:

- First read the item with a blank that needs to be filled.
- See if you can think of the answer even before you look at your choices.
- Even if the answer you first thought of is one of the choices, be sure to check the other choices. There may be an even better answer.
- For harder questions, try to fit every answer choice into the blank. Underline clue words that may help you find the correct answer. Write an **X** after answers that do not fit. Choose the answer that does fit. You can also use this strategy to double-check your answers.

Testing It Out

Now look at the sample question more closely.

Think: "Pablo was looking _____ to his family's camping trip." If I were going on a camping trip, I would probably be excited about it— looking forward to it. Maybe one of the choices is *forward*. Yes, it is— the answer must be **D**.

To double-check, I'll try the other answer choices in the sentence. None of them makes sense: "looking foremost," "looking forehead," and "looking former" all sound wrong. Answer **D** still seems correct to me.

True/False Questions

A true/false question asks you to read a statement and decide if it is right (true) or wrong (false). Sometimes you will be asked to write **T** for true or **F** for false. Most of the time you must fill in a bubble next to the correct answer.

EXAMPLE   **It is important to eat a good breakfast.**

(A) true

(B) false

To answer true/false questions on a test, think about the following:

• True/false sections contain more questions than other sections of a test. If there is a time limit on the test, you may need to go a little more quickly than usual. Do not spend too much time on any one question.

• First answer all of the easy questions. Circle the numbers next to harder ones and come back to them later.

• If you have time left after completing all the questions, quickly double-check your answers.

• True/false questions with words like *always*, *never*, *none*, *only*, and *every* are usually false. This is because they limit a statement so much.

• True-false questions with words like *most*, *many*, and *generally* are often true. This is because they make statements more believable.

Testing It Out

Now look at the sample question more closely.

Think: Is it important to eat a good breakfast? Yes, I've heard that before. I don't see any words like *always*, *never*, or *every* to limit the statement. My first instinct must be right. I'll choose **T** for true.

Matching Questions

Matching questions ask you to find pairs of words or phrases that go together. The choices are often shown in columns.

EXAMPLE	**Match items that mean the same, or almost the same, thing.**		
1 interest	A distress	1	Ⓐ Ⓑ Ⓒ Ⓓ
2 discourage	B cheer up	2	Ⓐ Ⓑ Ⓒ Ⓓ
3 encourage	C fascinate	3	Ⓐ Ⓑ Ⓒ Ⓓ
4 worry	D disappoint	4	Ⓐ Ⓑ Ⓒ Ⓓ

When answering matching questions on tests, follow these guidelines:

• Match the easiest choices first.
• If you come to a word you don't know, look for prefixes, suffixes, or root words to help figure out its meaning. Also, try using it in a sentence.
• Work down one column at a time. It is confusing to switch back and forth.

Testing It Out

Now look at the sample question more closely.

Think: I'll start with the first column. *Interest* is a word I've seen before. I think that *fascinate* means the same thing as, so I'll choose **C** to go with number 1.

I know that *disappointed* is the way people feel when they don't get something they want. *Let down* means the same thing. So I'll choose **D**.

I think that *support* may mean something similar to *help*. Let's see— "My mom gave me all the help she could." "My mom gave me all the support she could." Yes, both sentences make sense. I'll choose **B**.

The fourth word is *worry*. The only remaining choice is *distress*, but I don't know what it means. It might have something to do with being upset, but the only other possible word is *disappoint*, and I'm sure of my choice for that word. So I'll choose **A**.

Analogy Questions

Analogies are a special kind of question. In an analogy question, you are asked to figure out the relationship between two things. Then you must complete another pair with the same relationship.

EXAMPLE

Porcupine is to quills as bee is to _____ .

   Ⓐ sharp   Ⓒ buzzing

   Ⓑ insect   Ⓓ stinger

Analogies usually have two pairs of items. In the question above, the two pairs are *porcupine/quills* and *bee/ _____* . To answer analogy questions on standardized tests, do the following:

- Try to form a sentence that explains how they are related.
- Next, use your sentence to figure out the missing word in the second pair of items.
- For more difficult analogies, try each answer choice in the sentence you formed. Choose the answer that fits best.

Testing It Out

Now look at the sample question more closely.

Think: How are *porcupine* and *quills* related? A porcupine has quills on its body; it uses its quills to protect itself. So if I use the word *bee* in this sentence, I'd say, "A bee has a _____ on its body; it uses its _____ to protect itself."

Choice **A** is *sharp*. If I use *sharp* to complete the sentence, I end up with, *A bee has sharp on its body; it uses its sharp to protect itself.* That makes no sense.

Choice **B** is *insect*. If I use *insect* to complete the sentence, I end up with *A bee has an insect on its body; it uses its insect to protect itself.* That makes no sense, either.

Choice **C** is *buzzing*. *A bee has a buzzing on its body; it uses its buzzing to protect itself.* Bees do buzz, but they don't have *buzzing* on their body.

Choice **D** is *stinger*. *A bee has a stinger on its body; it uses its stinger to protect itself.* Yes, both parts of that sentence are true. **D** is the correct choice.

Short Answer Questions

Some test questions don't give you answers to choose from; instead, you must write short answers in your own words. These are called "short answer" or "open response" questions.

> **EXAMPLE** **Ted saw that a rowboat had tipped over and two people were struggling in the water. He swam out to the boat. He calmed the two swimmers and showed them how to hold on to the overturned boat. Then he stayed with them until a rescue boat could get there.**
>
> 1. What word or words would you use to describe Ted? _____
>
> 2. How do you think the people in the water felt about Ted? _____

When you must write short answers to questions on a standardized test, do the following:

- Read each question carefully. Make sure to respond directly to the question that is being asked.
- Your response should be short but complete.
- Write in complete sentences unless the directions say you don't have to.
- Make sure to double-check your answers for spelling, punctuation, and grammar when you are done.

Testing It Out

Now reread the paragraph about Ted and the questions.

 Think: From the story, I can tell that Ted is brave. He tried to save the swimmers even though it might have been dangerous. I know he is a good swimmer because he stayed in the water for a long time and showed the swimmers how to hold on to the boat. Even though the directions don't say, I know I should write in complete sentences. So I'll write:

1. *Ted is brave. He is also a good swimmer.*

The swimmers must have appreciated Ted's help. So I'll write:

2. *The swimmers were glad that Ted was there to help them.*

Name _____

Practice Test Answer Sheet

Fill in **only one** letter for each item. If you change an answer, make sure to erase your first mark completely.

Unit 1: Reading, pages 16-30

A Ⓐ Ⓑ Ⓒ Ⓓ	7 Ⓐ Ⓑ Ⓒ Ⓓ	15 Ⓐ Ⓑ Ⓒ Ⓓ	22 Ⓐ Ⓑ Ⓒ Ⓓ	29 Ⓕ Ⓖ Ⓗ Ⓙ
B Ⓕ Ⓖ Ⓗ Ⓙ	8 Ⓕ Ⓖ Ⓗ Ⓙ	16 Ⓕ Ⓖ Ⓗ Ⓙ	23 Ⓕ Ⓖ Ⓗ Ⓙ	30 Ⓐ Ⓑ Ⓒ Ⓓ
1 Ⓐ Ⓑ Ⓒ Ⓓ	9 Ⓐ Ⓑ Ⓒ Ⓓ	17 Ⓐ Ⓑ Ⓒ Ⓓ	24 Ⓐ Ⓑ Ⓒ Ⓓ	31 Ⓕ Ⓖ Ⓗ Ⓙ
2 Ⓕ Ⓖ Ⓗ Ⓙ	10 Ⓕ Ⓖ Ⓗ Ⓙ	18 Ⓕ Ⓖ Ⓗ Ⓙ	25 Ⓕ Ⓖ Ⓗ Ⓙ	32 Ⓐ Ⓑ Ⓒ Ⓓ
3 Ⓐ Ⓑ Ⓒ Ⓓ	11 Ⓐ Ⓑ Ⓒ Ⓓ	19 Ⓐ Ⓑ Ⓒ Ⓓ	26 Ⓐ Ⓑ Ⓒ Ⓓ	33 Ⓕ Ⓖ Ⓗ Ⓙ
4 Ⓕ Ⓖ Ⓗ Ⓙ	12 Ⓕ Ⓖ Ⓗ Ⓙ	20 Ⓕ Ⓖ Ⓗ Ⓙ	27 Ⓕ Ⓖ Ⓗ Ⓙ	34 Ⓐ Ⓑ Ⓒ Ⓓ
5 Ⓐ Ⓑ Ⓒ Ⓓ	13 Ⓐ Ⓑ Ⓒ Ⓓ	21 Ⓐ Ⓑ Ⓒ Ⓓ	D Ⓐ Ⓑ Ⓒ Ⓓ	
6 Ⓕ Ⓖ Ⓗ Ⓙ	14 Ⓕ Ⓖ Ⓗ Ⓙ	C Ⓐ Ⓑ Ⓒ Ⓓ	28 Ⓐ Ⓑ Ⓒ Ⓓ	

Unit 2: Language Arts, pages 31-41

A Ⓐ Ⓑ Ⓒ Ⓓ	9 Ⓐ Ⓑ Ⓒ Ⓓ	18 Ⓕ Ⓖ Ⓗ Ⓙ Ⓚ	25 Ⓐ Ⓑ Ⓒ Ⓓ	34 Ⓕ Ⓖ Ⓗ Ⓙ
1 Ⓐ Ⓑ Ⓒ Ⓓ	10 Ⓕ Ⓖ Ⓗ Ⓙ	19 Ⓐ Ⓑ Ⓒ Ⓓ Ⓔ	26 Ⓕ Ⓖ Ⓗ Ⓙ	35 Ⓐ Ⓑ Ⓒ Ⓓ
2 Ⓕ Ⓖ Ⓗ Ⓙ	C Ⓐ Ⓑ Ⓒ Ⓓ	20 Ⓕ Ⓖ Ⓗ Ⓙ	G Ⓐ Ⓑ Ⓒ Ⓓ Ⓔ	36 Ⓕ Ⓖ Ⓗ Ⓙ
B Ⓐ Ⓑ Ⓒ Ⓓ	11 Ⓐ Ⓑ Ⓒ Ⓓ	D Ⓐ Ⓑ Ⓒ Ⓓ	27 Ⓐ Ⓑ Ⓒ Ⓓ	37 Ⓐ Ⓑ Ⓒ Ⓓ
3 Ⓐ Ⓑ Ⓒ Ⓓ	12 Ⓕ Ⓖ Ⓗ Ⓙ	21 Ⓐ Ⓑ Ⓒ Ⓓ	28 Ⓕ Ⓖ Ⓗ Ⓙ	38 Ⓕ Ⓖ Ⓗ Ⓙ
4 Ⓕ Ⓖ Ⓗ Ⓙ	13 Ⓐ Ⓑ Ⓒ Ⓓ	22 Ⓕ Ⓖ Ⓗ Ⓙ	29 Ⓐ Ⓑ Ⓒ Ⓓ	39 Ⓐ Ⓑ Ⓒ Ⓓ
5 Ⓐ Ⓑ Ⓒ Ⓓ	14 Ⓕ Ⓖ Ⓗ Ⓙ Ⓚ	E Ⓐ Ⓑ Ⓒ Ⓓ Ⓔ	30 Ⓕ Ⓖ Ⓗ Ⓙ	40 Ⓕ Ⓖ Ⓗ Ⓙ Ⓚ
6 Ⓕ Ⓖ Ⓗ Ⓙ	15 Ⓐ Ⓑ Ⓒ Ⓓ Ⓔ	23 Ⓐ Ⓑ Ⓒ Ⓓ Ⓔ	31 Ⓐ Ⓑ Ⓒ Ⓓ	41 Ⓐ Ⓑ Ⓒ Ⓓ Ⓔ
7 Ⓐ Ⓑ Ⓒ Ⓓ	16 Ⓕ Ⓖ Ⓗ Ⓙ Ⓚ	24 Ⓕ Ⓖ Ⓗ Ⓙ Ⓚ	32 Ⓕ Ⓖ Ⓗ Ⓙ	42 Ⓕ Ⓖ Ⓗ Ⓙ Ⓚ
8 Ⓕ Ⓖ Ⓗ Ⓙ	17 Ⓐ Ⓑ Ⓒ Ⓓ Ⓔ	F Ⓐ Ⓑ Ⓒ Ⓓ	33 Ⓐ Ⓑ Ⓒ Ⓓ	43 Ⓐ Ⓑ Ⓒ Ⓓ Ⓔ

Unit 3: Mathematics, pages 42-51

A Ⓐ Ⓑ Ⓒ Ⓓ Ⓔ	6 Ⓕ Ⓖ Ⓗ Ⓙ Ⓚ	14 Ⓕ Ⓖ Ⓗ Ⓙ	21 Ⓐ Ⓑ Ⓒ Ⓓ Ⓔ	28 Ⓐ Ⓑ Ⓒ Ⓓ
B Ⓕ Ⓖ Ⓗ Ⓙ Ⓚ	7 Ⓐ Ⓑ Ⓒ Ⓓ Ⓔ	15 Ⓐ Ⓑ Ⓒ Ⓓ	22 Ⓕ Ⓖ Ⓗ Ⓙ Ⓚ	29 Ⓕ Ⓖ Ⓗ Ⓙ
1 Ⓐ Ⓑ Ⓒ Ⓓ Ⓔ	8 Ⓕ Ⓖ Ⓗ Ⓙ Ⓚ	16 Ⓕ Ⓖ Ⓗ Ⓙ Ⓚ	23 Ⓐ Ⓑ Ⓒ Ⓓ Ⓔ	30 Ⓐ Ⓑ Ⓒ Ⓓ
2 Ⓕ Ⓖ Ⓗ Ⓙ Ⓚ	9 Ⓐ Ⓑ Ⓒ Ⓓ Ⓔ	17 Ⓐ Ⓑ Ⓒ Ⓓ Ⓔ	D Ⓐ Ⓑ Ⓒ Ⓓ	31 Ⓕ Ⓖ Ⓗ Ⓙ
3 Ⓐ Ⓑ Ⓒ Ⓓ Ⓔ	10 Ⓕ Ⓖ Ⓗ Ⓙ	18 Ⓕ Ⓖ Ⓗ Ⓙ Ⓚ	24 Ⓐ Ⓑ Ⓒ Ⓓ	
4 Ⓕ Ⓖ Ⓗ Ⓙ Ⓚ	11 Ⓐ Ⓑ Ⓒ Ⓓ	E Ⓕ Ⓖ Ⓗ Ⓙ Ⓚ	25 Ⓕ Ⓖ Ⓗ Ⓙ	
C Ⓐ Ⓑ Ⓒ Ⓓ	12 Ⓕ Ⓖ Ⓗ Ⓙ	19 Ⓐ Ⓑ Ⓒ Ⓓ Ⓔ	26 Ⓐ Ⓑ Ⓒ Ⓓ	
5 Ⓐ Ⓑ Ⓒ Ⓓ	13 Ⓐ Ⓑ Ⓒ Ⓓ	20 Ⓕ Ⓖ Ⓗ Ⓙ Ⓚ	27 Ⓕ Ⓖ Ⓗ Ⓙ	

Name _____

Lesson 1   Reading Nonfiction

SAMPLE A

Did you ever hear about the "7–11 rule"? It's about something you use every day. Steps are supposed to have a tread—the part you step on—that is about 11 inches wide. The riser—the distance from one step to another—is supposed to be 7 inches high. Steps that use these dimensions are easiest to climb.

This passage is mostly about

> **A** the invention of steps.
>
> **B** exercising on steps.
>
> **C** things you use every day.
>
> **D** steps made the right way.

SAMPLE B

Find the word that best completes the sentence.

The ball _____ down the steps.

> **F** rolled   **H** rolling
>
> **G** roll   **J** having rolled

Be careful! There are two sets of letters for the answer choices. Skip difficult items and come back to them later. If you aren't sure which answer is correct, take your best guess.

Listening and Looking

It's amazing what you can learn by listening and looking. In this lesson, you will read about two interesting school projects that you might want to try.

GO

Test Prep

Name _____

Directions: Tomas keeps a journal for his All-Year Project in English. On the entry for this day, he wrote about an assignment one of his teachers had given him. Read the journal entry, then do numbers 1–6.

October 19

"Boy, does this sound like a goofy assignment," I said to Kendra, rolling my eyes. We were walking home after school talking about what Mr. Stewart had given us for homework this week. We were supposed to listen—just listen—for a total of two hours this week. We could do it any time we wanted, in short periods or long, and write down some of the things we heard. We also had to describe where we listened and the time of day.

As we walked by a small corner park, Kendra stopped for a moment and suggested, "Hey, I have an idea. Let's start right here. It's just about two-thirty, my parents won't be home for two more hours, and neither will your mother. We should just sit down in the park and get part of the assignment done. It will be a breeze."

For once, she had something. I told her it was a great idea, then spotted a bench beside the fountain. "Let's get started," I said.

We sat down and pulled out notebooks and pencils. After just a few seconds, Kendra began writing something down. I started right after her, and for the next half hour, we did nothing but sit, listen, and take notes.

GO

Name _____

Test Prep _____

At about three o'clock, Kendra said, "That's enough for me now. Do you want to compare notes? I want to be sure I did this right."

"Sure," I answered. "I can't believe all the things I heard. Maybe this isn't such a goofy assignment after all."

1 **About how long did Tomas and Kendra listen in the park?**

   A two hours

   B half an hour

   C a few seconds

   D a few minutes

2 **Kendra said the homework assignment would <u>be a breeze.</u>**
That means the assignment would be

hard.	long.	easy.	outside.
F	**G**	**H**	**J**

3 **The first sound Kendra probably wrote about is**

   A the fountain.   **C** crickets.

   B a fire engine.   **D** her watch.

GO

4 **Why did Mr. Stewart probably give the students this assignment?**

F It would be an easy way for them to get a good grade.

G It would give them a chance to work together.

H It would give them more free time for other assignments.

J It would help them understand the world around them better.

5 **Tomas and Kendra live in a city. Which of these sounds are they most likely to hear on the way home?**

A birds chirping

B the wind in the trees

C traffic sounds

D planes landing

6 **What lesson did Tomas probably learn?**

F Some assignments are better than they first seem.

G Kendra is a better student than he first thought.

H Mr. Stewart usually gives easy assignments.

J There is no reason to go right home after school.

GO

Name _____

Directions: For numbers 7 and 8, find the word that best completes the sentence.

7 **The water _____ in the fountain.**

   A splash   **C** splashing

   B having splashed   **D** splashed

8 **Kendra _____ a report next weekend.**

   F will write

   G wrote

   H having written

   J writing

9 **Find the simple predicate, or action word, of the sentence below.**

Two people listen better than one person.

  A   **B**   **C**   **D**

GO

Test Prep

Directions: This set of directions suggests an easy project for a class of students or even a whole school. Read the directions to find out how you can get an "up close and personal" view of birds. Then do numbers 10–21.

Birds: Up Close and Personal

Many schools and communities now have small nature areas. These nature areas have a bird feeder of some kind. If the nature area in your community has a feeder, try this observation activity. If not, try setting one up in your school! The activity works best when a number of students are involved, and it can continue from year to year.

1. Find a spot that is close enough to the feeder to see the birds but not so close that you scare them away. Binoculars will help you get a better look at the birds.

2. Throughout the day, keep a record of the birds that are at the feeder. Note the type of bird and how many there are of each kind. If possible, observe the feeder at the same time each day.

3. Create a "lifetime list" of birds that appear at the feeder. This could be a wall chart with the name of each bird that appears at the feeder. In addition, keep a detailed notebook showing the results of each observation.

This activity can lead to many other projects. For example, you can create a computer database showing the kind and number of birds that come to the feeder throughout the year. It's also possible to do an in-depth study of bird families, or identify times of the day that are best for observing different kinds of birds.

GO

Name _____

10 **This passage is mostly about**

    F feeding birds.

    G observing birds.

    H building a bird feeder.

    J bird migrations.

11 **In this picture, students are probably**

    A putting seed in a feeder.

    B taking notes about birds.

    C observing birds.

    D making a lifetime list.

12 **Binoculars are important because they let you**

    F choose the right seed.

    G organize your notes.

    H take good notes.

    J observe birds closely.

13 **It is important to look at the birds at the same time each day so you can**

    A make comparisons from day to day.

    B get to all your classes on time.

    C meet the same friends each day.

    D talk about birds with your teacher.

GO

14 In the text, a "lifetime list" of birds is a

    F book.   **H** wall chart.

    G computer program.   **J** journal.

15 Find the sentence that best completes this description of a bird.

This bird was about the size of a robin. _____ . I saw it near a pond.

    A My friends and I go there often.

    B Birds seem to be more active in the morning.

    C It was mostly black with red marks on its wings.

    D Robins fly south in the winter.

16 The last sentence in the introduction is about

    F collecting information.

    G drawing conclusions.

    H comparing different birds.

    J sharing information.

17 Find the sentence that is complete and correctly written.

    A To take good notes.

    B Some birds feed early.

    C Using a computer.

    D A detailed wall chart.

GO

Name _____

18 **Find the word that fits in both sentences.**

What _____ will you be on vacation?
I enjoy eating _____ .

F days

H weeks

G fruit

J dates

19 **Find the sentence that has correct capitalization and punctuation.**

A my sister takes good notes.

C What kind of bird was that?

B This is a good bird book

D Did you put seed in the feeder.

20 **Choose the sentence that best combines these two sentences into one.**

A bird landed on a tree.
The tree was an apple tree.

F The bird landed on an apple tree.

G The bird landed and it landed on an apple tree.

H On an apple tree the bird landed.

J An apple tree, on which the bird landed.

21 **Choose the sentences that best support this topic sentence.**

Birds eat many different things.

A Their colors vary from drab to colorful. Some drab birds have small patches of color.

B Small birds generally eat seeds and insects. Larger birds eat small animals and even fish.

C They also fly in different ways. Gulls soar, but hummingbirds flap their wings often.

D Even in cities, birds can survive. Some hawks now make their homes in skyscrapers.

GO

Name _____

Lesson 2 **Reading Fiction**

Family Traditions

Many families have traditions that are their very own. Think about your family. You probably have some traditions that are so natural you don't think about them anymore.

Buster was the neighborhood cat. His favorite spot was on Mrs. Wilson's car. He sat on the hood while everyone walked by and petted him.

This story suggests that Buster is

A cautious.

C friendly.

B large.

D curious.

Skim the story then read the questions. Look back at the story to find the answers. Some questions won't be answered directly in the story. Answer the easiest questions first.

Directions: Here is a story about an unusual family tradition. Read the story and then do numbers 22 and 23.

The Un-Birthday

In my family we don't celebrate birthdays. At least we don't celebrate them like most families. My friends say I have an "un-birthday."

The tradition started with my grandmother. She and grandfather grew up in Poland. They escaped before World War II and made their way to America. When they got here, they were so grateful that they decided to share what they had with others. On their birthdays, they gave each other just one small gift. Then they each bought a gift for someone who needed it more than they did.

GO

Name _____

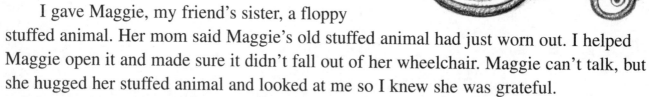

As the years passed and the family grew, the tradition continued. On my last birthday, I got a backpack for school. We had a little party with cake and all of that, and then we headed off to the Lionel School. This is a school for kids who are disabled. Some of the children are in electric wheelchairs, and only a few can walk. I picked this school out because one of my friends has a sister there.

When we walked in with our arms full of gifts, the kids were really excited. Even though we gave them just little things—sticker books, puzzles, that sort of thing—all the presents were wrapped and had bows.

I gave Maggie, my friend's sister, a floppy stuffed animal. Her mom said Maggie's old stuffed animal had just worn out. I helped Maggie open it and made sure it didn't fall out of her wheelchair. Maggie can't talk, but she hugged her stuffed animal and looked at me so I knew she was grateful.

I don't get as much stuff as my friends, but I don't feel bad, even though I want a new skateboard. I have enough stuff, probably too much. Seeing Maggie and the other kids receive their gifts was a lot better than getting a bunch of presents myself.

22   This passage is mostly about

   A   a child's disappointing birthday.

   B   a school for disabled children.

   C   a family that lives in Poland.

   D   an unusual birthday tradition.

23   What does the family do to show they want the children at the Lionel School to feel important?

   F   drive to the school   **H**   have just a small party

   G   wrap the presents carefully   **J**   give them small gifts

GO

Test Prep

Name _____

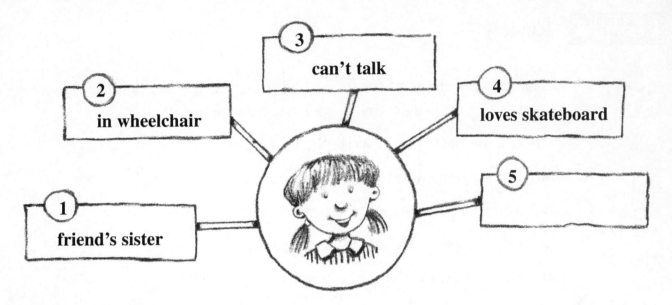

Directions: Use this web about the passage to do numbers 24 and 25.

24 **Which phrase would best fit in Box 5?**

  A shows gratitude

  B learns to read

  C drops stuffed animal

  D grew up in Poland

25 **Which box contains information that does not belong in the web?**

  F Box 1

  G Box 2

  H Box 4

  J Box 5

Directions: For numbers 26 and 27, choose the sentence that is written correctly.

26 **A** the party will happen last week.

  B the presents was all wrapped.

  C Maggie will soon learn to read.

  D The kids at the school excited.

27 **F** he doesn't celebrate birthdays.

  G She don't have a party.

  H Got one gift.

  J She hugged her stuffed animal.

STOP

Name _____

Lesson 3 Review

SAMPLE
D

[1]Natural fires are good for forests. [2]Burning dead wood and heavy brush. [3]This helps new trees and grass grow better.

Choose the best way to write Sentence 2.

A Having burned dead wood and heavy brush.

B They burn dead wood and heavy brush.

C Dead wood and heavy brush they burn.

D Dead wood will burn heavy brush.

Directions: Greg is writing a story for the Young Author's column of the school paper. The first draft of the story needs some editing. Here is the first part of the story.

> [1]Our town's name is Lost City. [2]It has an unusual history. [3]First of all, it was founded in 1886 by accident. [4]A group of pioneers thought they were headed toward San Francisco. [5]Instead, they ended up hundreds of miles farther up the coast.

28 **Which of these best combines Sentences 1 and 2 into one sentence?**

A Lost City has an unusual history and it is our town.

B An unusual history, our town is Lost City.

C Our town, Lost City, has an unusual history.

D With an unusual history, our town is Lost City.

29 **Which is the best way to write Sentence 4?**

F A group of pioneers toward San Francisco were headed.

G Toward San Francisco a group of pioneers thought they were headed.

H San Francisco, they thought the pioneers were headed.

J Best as it is

GO

Name _____

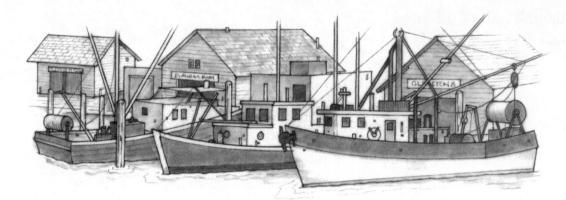

Now read the next part of the story.

[1]The founders of Lost City from Baltimore came. [2]They knew about fishing, trapping crabs, and gathering oysters and clams. [3]It was only natural that they would use their skills in the Pacific Ocean. [4]Soon, Lost City was known for its fine seafood. [5]Wagons packed with ice and snow brought fish, oysters, and crabs to inland towns. [6]Seafood restaurants were on almost every corner.

30 Select the best way to write Sentence 1.

A The founders of Lost City came from Baltimore.

B From Baltimore the founders of Lost City came.

C Coming from Baltimore were the founders of Lost City.

D Best as it is

31 Choose the best way to write Sentence 4.

F Lost City was known soon for its fine seafood.

G For its fine seafood, Lost City was known soon.

H Lost City, for its fine seafood, was soon known.

J Best as it is

GO

This is the last part of the story.

> ¹The sleepy little fishing town doubled in size almost overnight. ²Harriet Johnson decided to build a resort on the cliffs near the beach. ³With her fortune, she hired hundreds of workers to complete the job. ⁴Many of them decided to stay when the job was finished. ⁵The workers lived in tents on the beach. ⁶These workers the logging industry that exists even today helped build.

32 **Choose the sentence that does not belong in the paragraph.**

A Sentence 2   **C** Sentence 4

B Sentence 3   **D** Sentence 5

33 **Select the best way to write Sentence 6.**

F The workers in the logging industry that exists today helped build.

G These workers, they helped build the logging industry. It exists even today.

H These workers helped build the logging industry that exists even today.

J Best as it is

Greg's friend, Betty, wrote a paragraph about the school play.

34 **Find the sentence that best completes Betty's story.**

The junior high play will take place on Friday and Saturday nights. _____ .
The play will be held in the school auditorium.

A Tryouts were last month.   **C** My sister likes plays.

B Tickets cost $2.50 per person.   **D** Did you like it?

STOP

Name _____

Lesson 1   Vocabulary

Directions: For Sample A and numbers 1 and 2, choose the word that correctly completes both sentences.

Directions: For Sample B and numbers 3 and 4, choose the word that means the **opposite** of the underlined word.

SAMPLE A

The player began to _____ .
Put the new _____ on the car.

A   run

B   fender

C   weaken

D   tire

SAMPLE B

recall information

A   forget

B   remember

C   write

D   find

1   The sun _____ at 5:45.
A _____ grew beside the steps.

A   appeared

B   rose

C   flower

D   set

2   My _____ is in the closet.
Add a new _____ of paint.

F   hat

G   color

H   shirt

J   coat

3   valuable painting

A   strange

B   expensive

C   worthless

D   humorous

4   left promptly

F   late

G   recently

H   quietly

J   slowly

Try each answer choice in BOTH blanks. Use the meaning of a sentence to find the answer.

GO

Name _____

Directions: For number 5, read the sentence with the missing word and the question about that word. Choose the word that best answers the question.

5 Let's _____ the ripe apples. Which word means to gather the ripe apples?

  A eat

  B collect

  C check

  D sell

Directions: For numbers 6 and 7, choose the word that means the same, or about the same, as the underlined word.

6 fast <u>vehicle</u>

  F runner   **H** car

  G animal   **J** computer

7 baggy <u>trousers</u>

  A shirt   **C** clothes

  B pants   **D** coat

Directions: For numbers 8–10, read the paragraph. For each numbered blank, there is a list of words with the same number. Choose the word from each list that best completes the meaning of the paragraph.

Glass is an amazing substance. Made by heating sand with a few other simple chemicals, glass is both useful and beautiful. In the __(8)__ you drink your juice in a glass. At your school, you may __(9)__ the building through a glass door. The lights inside the school are made of glass, as is the screen of the computer you will use. If you go to gym class, the basketball backboard might even be made of glass. Your family may have pieces of glass as decorations around the house, and if you go to a museum, you might see __(10)__ glass from hundreds of years ago.

8 **F** evening   **H** morning

  G time   **J** mood

10 **F** new   **H** full

  G antique   **J** broken

9 **A** open   **C** like

  B see   **D** enter

STOP

Name _____

Lesson 2 Language Mechanics

SAMPLE C

Directions: Choose the answer that is written correctly and shows the correct capitalization and punctuation.

A Rudy gave janet a gift.

B We can leave now but, the party isn't until seven.

C Do you think she will be surprised?

D This cake looks wonderful?

Be sure you know if you are to look for correct or incorrect capitalization and punctuation.

Directions: For numbers 11 and 12, decide which punctuation mark, if any, is needed in the sentence.

11 **The puppy couldn't find the food dish**

, . ? None

A **B** **C** **D**

12 **"This is fun, answered Lettie.**

, ? " None

F **G** **H** **J**

Directions: For numbers 13 and 14, choose the answer that is written correctly and shows the correct capitalization and punctuation.

13 **A** The tennis courts are full

   B Venus put our names on the list.

   C Did you remember your racket.

   D This can of tennis balls is new?

14 **F** Tell Mrs Jensen I called.

   G Miss. Richards will be late.

   H Our coach is Mr. Wanamaker

   J Dr. Cullinane was here earlier.

GO

Name _____

Directions: For numbers 15–20, look at the underlined part of the sentence. Choose the answer that shows the best capitalization and punctuation for that part.

15 **Winters are warm in Tucson Arizona.**

  A Tucson, arizona

  B Tucson Arizona,

  C Tucson, Arizona.

  D Correct as it is

16 **The play will be held on Wednesday, Thursday, and Friday, nights.**

  F Thursday, and Friday

  G Thursday, and, Friday

  H Thursday and Friday,

  J Correct as it is

(17) January 5 2001,

(18) dear Burt

    My mom said you are coming to see us next month.

(19) If the weather is right, we can go skiing, sledding, or ice skating. You can borrow my brother's skis and skates.

    See you soon.

        (20) Your Cousin,

          Sarah

17 **A** January 5, 2001

    B January 5 2001

    C January 5, 2001,

    D Correct as it is

18 **F** Dear Burt

    G dear burt

    H Dear Burt,

    J Correct as it is

19 **A** skiing sledding or

    B skiing, sledding, or,

    C skiing sledding or,

    D Correct as it is

20 **F** Your Cousin

    G Your cousin,

    H your Cousin,

    J Correct as it is

STOP

Name _____

Lesson 3 Spelling

Directions: For Sample D and numbers 21 and 22, choose the word that is spelled correctly and best completes the sentence.

Directions: For Sample E and numbers 23 and 24, read each phrase. Find the underlined word that is <u>not</u> spelled correctly. If all words are spelled correctly, mark "All correct."

SAMPLE D   Harry wrote a _____ to the paper.

   A leter   **C** ledder

   B lettir   **D** letter

SAMPLE E
  A college <u>dormitory</u>

  B <u>assemble</u> a toy

  C <u>loyal</u> dog

  D <u>pause</u> briefly

  E All correct

21 Tomorrow will be _____ .

  A rainee

  B rainie

  C ranie

  D rainy

22 Did you finish the _____ yet?

  F lesson

  G leson

  H lessin

  J lessan

23 **A** <u>lene</u> meat

  B <u>demonstrate</u> a toy

  C <u>reflect</u> light

  D <u>terrible</u> food

  E All correct

24 **F** make me <u>yawn</u>

  G <u>wooden</u> bench

  H <u>accidentally</u> drop it

  J <u>ajust</u> the radio

  K All correct

Don't spend too much time looking at the words. Pretty soon, they all begin to look like they are spelled wrong.

STOP

Name _____

Lesson 4 Writing

Directions: Read the paragraph about a book one student really liked. Then write one or two sentences to answer each question below.

> I really liked the book *The Wizard of Oz* and think others will like it, too. It was very exciting, especially the part where Dorothy went to the Wicked Witch's castle and made the Witch melt. I also liked the way the characters worked together to solve their problems. Finally when Dorothy says, "There's no place like home," I thought about my home and the many wonderful things I have.

Think of a book you really liked. What is its title?

_____

_____

_____

Why do you think others should read it?

_____

_____

_____

What are some specific parts of the book that you think others would enjoy?

_____

_____

_____

GO

Name _____

Directions: Read the short story about one child's problem. Then think about a fiction story that you would like to write. Write one or two sentences to answer each question below.

> Shandra kicked a rock. She shook her head. She had missed the bus again, and she knew she'd be late for school.
>
> That night, Shandra set two alarms. She put them on the other side of her room. She asked her friend to call her to make sure she was up.
>
> The next morning Shandra was smiling. For once, she would be on-time with everyone else.

Think about the main character. Who is it? What is he or she like? Why are you writing about this character?

_____

_____

_____

What is the setting of the story?

_____

_____

What kind of problem will the main character have? How will the character solve the problem?

_____

_____

_____

_____

STOP

Name _____

Lesson 5 Review

Directions: For Sample F and numbers 25 and 26, read the sentences with the missing word and the question about that word. Choose the word that best answers the question.

SAMPLE F

The owner had to _____ the puppy for chewing the shoes.
Which word means to speak harshly to the puppy?

  A scold   **C** alert

  B pursue   **D** inspire

25 **We hiked to a _____ campsite.**
Which word means the campsite was far away?

  A remote   **C** crowded

  B pleasant   **D** level

26 **The bird _____ from branch to branch.**
Which word means to fly quickly from branch to branch?

  F coasted

  G hopped

  H darted

  J paced

SAMPLE G
Directions: Find the underlined word that is <u>not</u> spelled correctly.

  A avoid <u>capture</u>

  B hate to <u>complane</u>

  C <u>empty</u> room

  D <u>fourteen</u> points

  E All correct

Directions: For number 27, choose the word that means the **opposite** of the underlined word.

27 **<u>rough</u> board**

  A large

  B heavy

  C smooth

  D long

Directions: For number 28, choose the word that means the same, or about the same, as the underlined word.

28 **attend a <u>conference</u>**

  F party

  G game

  H meeting

  J race

GO

Name _____

Directions: For number 29, decide which punctuation mark, if any, is needed in the sentence.

29   The clouds were dark and the wind was getting stronger.

     !   .   ?   None

    A   **B**   **C**   **D**

Directions: For numbers 30 and 31, choose the answer that is written correctly and shows the correct capitalization and punctuation.

30 **F** Suzie whispered, "This is a great movie."

     G "Don't forget your money said Mother."

     H Are there seats up front?" asked Bruce?

     J "Let's get popcorn" suggested Wanda.

31 **A** Dad bought seeds plants, and fertilizer.

     B The shovel rake and hoe are in the garage.

     C We usually camp with Jan, Bob and, Annie.

     D The garden had corn, beans, and peas.

Directions: For numbers 32–35, look at the underlined part of the paragraph. Choose the answer that shows the best capitalization and punctuation for that part.

(32)   Ricky <u>said, "Watch</u> what I can do." He rode his
(33)   bike to the middle of the <u>driveway. And</u> balanced himself
(34)   on the back wheel. <u>Il'1 bet</u> there isn't another kid in
(35)   <u>mayfield who</u> can do that.

32 **F** said, Watch

     G said, "watch

     H said "Watch

     J Correct as it is

33 **A** driveway and

     B driveway and,

     C driveway And

     D Correct as it is

34 **F** Ill bet

     G Ill' bet

     H I'll bet

     J Correct as it is

35 **A** mayfield. Who

     B Mayfield who

     C mayfield, who

     D Correct as it is

GO

Name _____

Directions: For numbers 36–39, choose the word that is spelled correctly and best completes the sentence.

36 The _____ is narrow here.

　F　channel

　G　channle

　H　chanel

　J　chanell

37 Do you like _____ movies?

　A　horrorr

　B　horor

　C　horror

　D　horrer

38 Three _____ people lived in the city.

　F　milion

　G　millun

　H　millione

　J　million

39 The train _____ arrived.

　A　finaly

　B　finnaly

　C　finely

　D　finally

Directions: For numbers 40–43, read each phrase. Find the underlined word that is <u>not</u> spelled correctly. If all the underlined words are spelled correctly, mark "All correct."

40 F　smart <u>dicision</u>

　G　<u>favorite</u> teacher

　H　<u>gather</u> wood

　J　famous <u>legend</u>

　K　All correct

41 A　<u>hardest</u> job

　B　<u>invite</u> them

　C　this <u>month</u>

　D　too much <u>luggage</u>

　E　All correct

42 F　daring <u>rescue</u>

　G　<u>solid</u> rock

　H　<u>oister</u> shell

　J　blue <u>plastic</u>

　K　All correct

43 A　A <u>certain</u> number

　B　good <u>citizen</u>

　C　<u>ceiling</u> fan

　D　<u>Wenesday</u> night

　E　All correct

GO

Name _____

Directions: Read the flyer that two girls designed to advertise their landscaping business. Then think about what you could do around your neighborhood to make money. Write one or two sentences to answer each question below.

Hire us
to take care of your
yard this summer.

We will mow, edge, water, and care for your flowers. Our prices are reasonable. We work hard. We can give you letters from other neighbors who have used our yard services. Call for more information!

Tina and Yani
123-4567

Pick one thing you could do around your neighborhood to make money. Describe what you would do.

_____

_____

_____

Why should your neighbors hire you to do this for them?

_____

_____

_____

How would you convince your neighbors to hire you?

_____

_____

_____

STOP

Name _____

Lesson 1 Computation

SAMPLE A

$$31 \atop +\,25$$

A   6

B   56

C   54

D   46

E   None of these

SAMPLE B

$3\overline{)90}$

F   20

G   40

H   87

J   93

K   None of these

TIPS

Look carefully at the operation sign.
Work neatly on scratch paper.

1

$$78 \atop +\,46$$

A   32

B   114

C   122

D   124

E   None of these

3

A   328

B   1296

C   320

D   1396

E   None of these

2

$$0.4 \atop -\,0.4$$

F   0

G   0.8

H   0.04

J   1

K   None of these

4

$182 \div 5 =$

F   36

G   36 R2

H   32

J   30 R2

K   None of these

STOP

Name _____

Lesson 2 Mathematics Skills

SAMPLE C Which of these number sentences would help you find the total number of flags?

A 5 + 3 = ☐   **C** 5 × 3 = ☐

B 5 − 3 = ☐   **D** 5 ÷ 3 = ☐

Read the problem carefully. Look for key words, numbers, and figures.

Think about what you are supposed to do before you start working.

Stay with your first answer. Change it only if you are sure it is wrong and another answer is better.

Name _____

The Community Pool

Directions: The town of Middlebury opened a community pool with a snack bar last year. Do numbers 5–9 about the pool.

5   The only charge to use the pool is the $3 parking charge. Which of these number sentences should be used to find how much money the parking lot made on a day when 82 cars were parked there?

   A $82 + 3 =$

   B $82 - 3 =$

   C $82 \times 3 =$

   D $82 \div 3 =$

6   To be allowed into the deep end of the pool, children must swim 12 laps across the shallow end without stopping. If Jessica has completed 8 laps, how many more laps must she swim to pass the test?

   F 3

   G 4

   H 8

   J 12

   K None of these

GO

7 Last week, the snack bar sold 1024 hot dogs. This week, it sold 1155 hot dogs. What was the total number of hot dogs served for the two weeks?

A 131

B 1179

C 2079

D 2179

E None of these

8 The 4th grade had their class party at the pool. There are 120 4th graders, but 5 were absent that day. How many students attended the class party?

F 115

G 125

H 24

J 105

K None of these

9 Ms. Fava divided her class of 24 students into groups of 2 students so that each child would have a buddy. How many groups of 2 students were there?

A 2

B 48

C 12

D 22

E None of these

GO

Name _____

Directions: For numbers 10–12, you do not need to find exact answers. Use estimation to choose the best answer.

10 **Which of these is the best estimate of 767 ÷ 7 =   ?**

   F 10

   G 11

   H 100

   J 110

11 **Use estimation to find which problem will have the greatest answer.**

   A   357   **C**   888
        – 63   – 666

   B   615   **D**   915
       – 485   – 769

12 **Leah is making an orange punch recipe in a very large punch bowl. Orange juice comes in different-sized containers. Which sized container should she buy in order to purchase the fewest number of containers?**

   F A one-cup container

   G A one-gallon container

   H A one-pint container

   J A one-quart container

GO

Name _____

13 Juan kept a log of the number of minutes he spent practicing the trumpet for the past three weeks. Which is the best estimate of the number of minutes he practiced during that time period?

A 200

B 300

C 400

D 500

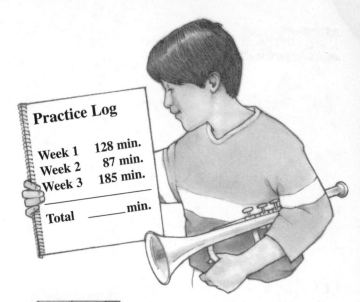

Practice Log

Week 1   128 min.
Week 2   87 min.
Week 3   185 min.

Total _____ min.

14 Which of these shows the top view of the figure above?

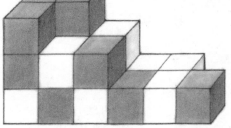

   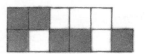   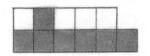   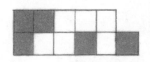

F   **G**   **H**   **J**

15 Use the ruler at the right to help you solve this problem.
Which of these paper clips is approximately 2 inches long?

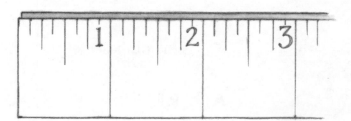

        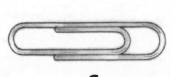   

A   **B**   **C**   **D**

STOP

Name _____

Lesson 3   Review

16

$$6.89$$
$$+3.00$$

F   3.89

G   3.98

H   0.88

J   9.89

K   None of these

17

$$925$$
$$-\ \ 6$$

A   919

B   931

C   4650

D   4660

E   None of these

18

$5 \times 40 =$

F   45

G   240

H   450

J   540

K   None of these

19

$15\overline{)90}$

A   5 R4

B   6

C   8

D   8 R4

E   None of these

20

$$794$$
$$-318$$

F   384

G   484

H   476

J   1112

K   None of these

21

$$\frac{4}{7}$$
$$+\frac{3}{7}$$

A $\frac{1}{7}$

B $\frac{5}{7}$

C $\frac{6}{7}$

D   1

E   None of these

22

$$132$$
$$\times\ \ 4$$

F   528

G   136

H   478

J   476

K   None of these

23

$$125$$
$$-\ 19$$

A   144

B   124

C   106

D   116

E   None of these

GO

Name _____

SAMPLE D

150 □ 6 =

Look at the problem above. Which of these symbols goes in the box to get the smallest answer?

    A +   **C** ×

    B −   **D** ÷

24 Kim made one straight cut across the trapezoid. Which pair of figures could be the two cut pieces of the trapezoid?

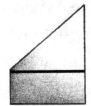

A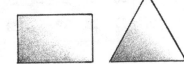

C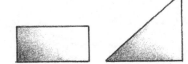

B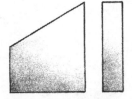

D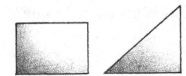

25 Look at the thermometers. How did the temperature change between Saturday and Sunday? On Sunday it was

    F 5 degrees cooler than on Saturday.

    G 10 degrees cooler than on Saturday.

    H 5 degrees warmer than on Saturday.

    J 10 degrees warmer than on Saturday.

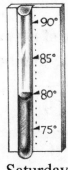
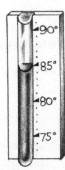

Saturday   Sunday

GO

Name _____

School Olympics

Directions: The fourth grade has School Olympics after the last day of school. Do numbers 26–31.

Make sure you are on number 26 on your answer sheet.

26 **The School Olympics start the Tuesday after school ends. If school ends on Friday, May 30, on what date do the School Olympics begin?**

   A May 31

   B June 1

   C June 2

   D June 3

27 **Yusef is in line to take his turn at the long jump. There are 13 people in line and he is in the middle. What is his place in line?**

   F fifth

   G tenth

   H seventh

   J sixth

28 **There are an even number of events in which students can participate. Which of these could be the number of events?**

23	19	24	31
A	**B**	**C**	**D**

GO

Directions: The graph shows how many students participated in certain events. Study the graph. Then do numbers 29–31.

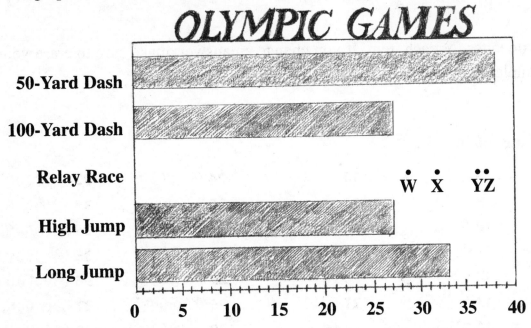

29 In which two events did the same number of students participate?

F 50-yard dash and high jump

G 50-yard dash and long jump

H 100-yard dash and high jump

J long jump and high jump

30 After this graph was made, 4 students switched from the 50-yard dash to the high jump. How many students then competed in the high jump?

A 29

B 30

C 31

D 33

31 The graph is not complete. There are 28 students who competed in the relay race. Which point should the bar be drawn to?

F Point W

G Point X

H Point Y

J Point Z

STOP

Name _____

Final Test Answer Sheet

Fill in **only one** letter for each item. If you change an answer, make sure to erase your first mark completely.

Unit 1: Reading, pages 54-59

A Ⓐ Ⓑ Ⓒ Ⓓ	**8** Ⓕ Ⓖ Ⓗ Ⓙ	**16** Ⓕ Ⓖ Ⓗ Ⓙ	**24** Ⓐ Ⓑ Ⓒ Ⓓ	**32** Ⓐ Ⓑ Ⓒ Ⓓ
1 Ⓐ Ⓑ Ⓒ Ⓓ	**9** Ⓐ Ⓑ Ⓒ Ⓓ	**17** Ⓐ Ⓑ	**25** Ⓕ Ⓖ Ⓗ Ⓙ	**33** Ⓐ Ⓑ Ⓒ Ⓓ
2 Ⓕ Ⓖ Ⓗ Ⓙ	**10** Ⓕ Ⓖ Ⓗ Ⓙ	**18** Ⓐ Ⓑ	**26** Ⓐ Ⓑ	**34** Ⓐ Ⓑ Ⓒ Ⓓ
3 Ⓐ Ⓑ Ⓒ Ⓓ	**11** Ⓐ Ⓑ Ⓒ Ⓓ	**19** Ⓐ Ⓑ	**27** Ⓐ Ⓑ	**35** Ⓐ Ⓑ Ⓒ Ⓓ
4 Ⓕ Ⓖ Ⓗ Ⓙ	**12** Ⓕ Ⓖ Ⓗ Ⓙ	**20** Ⓐ Ⓑ	**28** Ⓐ Ⓑ Ⓒ Ⓓ	**36** Ⓕ Ⓖ Ⓗ Ⓙ
5 Ⓐ Ⓑ Ⓒ Ⓓ	**13** Ⓐ Ⓑ Ⓒ Ⓓ	**21** Ⓐ Ⓑ	**29** Ⓕ Ⓖ Ⓗ Ⓙ	**37** Ⓕ Ⓖ Ⓗ Ⓙ
6 Ⓕ Ⓖ Ⓗ Ⓙ	**14** Ⓕ Ⓖ Ⓗ Ⓙ	**22** Ⓐ Ⓑ Ⓒ Ⓓ	**30** Ⓐ Ⓑ Ⓒ Ⓓ	**38** Ⓕ Ⓖ Ⓗ Ⓙ
7 Ⓐ Ⓑ Ⓒ Ⓓ	**15** Ⓐ Ⓑ Ⓒ Ⓓ	**23** Ⓕ Ⓖ Ⓗ Ⓙ	**31** Ⓕ Ⓖ Ⓗ Ⓙ	**39** Ⓕ Ⓖ Ⓗ Ⓙ

Unit 2: Language Arts, pages 60-68

A Ⓐ Ⓑ Ⓒ Ⓓ	**11** Ⓐ Ⓑ Ⓒ Ⓓ	**22** Ⓕ Ⓖ Ⓗ Ⓙ	**33** Ⓐ Ⓑ Ⓒ Ⓓ	**44** Ⓕ Ⓖ Ⓗ Ⓙ
1 Ⓐ Ⓑ Ⓒ Ⓓ	**12** Ⓕ Ⓖ Ⓗ Ⓙ	**23** Ⓐ Ⓑ Ⓒ Ⓓ	**34** Ⓕ Ⓖ Ⓗ Ⓙ	**45** Ⓐ Ⓑ Ⓒ Ⓓ
2 Ⓕ Ⓖ Ⓗ Ⓙ	**13** Ⓐ Ⓑ Ⓒ Ⓓ	**24** Ⓕ Ⓖ Ⓗ Ⓙ	**35** Ⓐ Ⓑ Ⓒ Ⓓ	**46** Ⓕ Ⓖ Ⓗ Ⓙ
3 Ⓐ Ⓑ Ⓒ Ⓓ	**14** Ⓕ Ⓖ Ⓗ Ⓙ Ⓚ	**25** Ⓐ Ⓑ Ⓒ Ⓓ	**36** Ⓕ Ⓖ Ⓗ Ⓙ	**47** Ⓐ Ⓑ Ⓒ Ⓓ
4 Ⓕ Ⓖ Ⓗ Ⓙ	**15** Ⓐ Ⓑ Ⓒ Ⓓ Ⓔ	**26** Ⓕ Ⓖ Ⓗ Ⓙ	**37** Ⓐ Ⓑ Ⓒ Ⓓ	**48** Ⓕ Ⓖ Ⓗ Ⓙ
5 Ⓐ Ⓑ Ⓒ Ⓓ	**16** Ⓕ Ⓖ Ⓗ Ⓙ Ⓚ	**27** Ⓐ Ⓑ Ⓒ Ⓓ	**38** Ⓕ Ⓖ Ⓗ Ⓙ	**49** Ⓐ Ⓑ Ⓒ Ⓓ
6 Ⓕ Ⓖ Ⓗ Ⓙ	**17** Ⓐ Ⓑ Ⓒ Ⓓ Ⓔ	**28** Ⓕ Ⓖ Ⓗ Ⓙ	**39** Ⓐ Ⓑ Ⓒ Ⓓ	**50** Ⓕ Ⓖ Ⓗ Ⓙ
7 Ⓐ Ⓑ Ⓒ Ⓓ	**18** Ⓕ Ⓖ Ⓗ Ⓙ	**29** Ⓐ Ⓑ Ⓒ Ⓓ	**40** Ⓕ Ⓖ Ⓗ Ⓙ	**51** Ⓐ Ⓑ Ⓒ Ⓓ
8 Ⓕ Ⓖ Ⓗ Ⓙ	**19** Ⓐ Ⓑ Ⓒ Ⓓ Ⓔ	**30** Ⓕ Ⓖ Ⓗ Ⓙ	**41** Ⓐ Ⓑ Ⓒ Ⓓ	
9 Ⓐ Ⓑ Ⓒ Ⓓ	**20** Ⓕ Ⓖ Ⓗ Ⓙ	**31** Ⓐ Ⓑ Ⓒ Ⓓ	**42** Ⓕ Ⓖ Ⓗ Ⓙ	
10 Ⓕ Ⓖ Ⓗ Ⓙ	**21** Ⓐ Ⓑ Ⓒ Ⓓ	**32** Ⓕ Ⓖ Ⓗ Ⓙ	**43** Ⓐ Ⓑ Ⓒ Ⓓ	

GO

Test Prep

Name _____

Final Test Answer Sheet

Fill in **only one** letter for each item. If you change an answer, make sure to erase your first mark completely.

Unit 3: Mathematics, pages 69-77

1 Ⓐ Ⓑ Ⓒ Ⓓ Ⓔ	10 Ⓕ Ⓖ Ⓗ Ⓙ	20 Ⓕ Ⓖ Ⓗ Ⓙ	30 Ⓕ Ⓖ Ⓗ Ⓙ	40 Ⓕ Ⓖ Ⓗ Ⓙ
2 Ⓕ Ⓖ Ⓗ Ⓙ Ⓚ	11 Ⓐ Ⓑ Ⓒ Ⓓ	21 Ⓐ Ⓑ Ⓒ Ⓓ	31 Ⓐ Ⓑ Ⓒ Ⓓ	41 Ⓐ Ⓑ Ⓒ Ⓓ
3 Ⓐ Ⓑ Ⓒ Ⓓ Ⓔ	12 Ⓕ Ⓖ Ⓗ Ⓙ	22 Ⓕ Ⓖ Ⓗ Ⓙ	32 Ⓕ Ⓖ Ⓗ Ⓙ	42 Ⓕ Ⓖ Ⓗ Ⓙ
4 Ⓕ Ⓖ Ⓗ Ⓙ Ⓚ	13 Ⓐ Ⓑ Ⓒ Ⓓ	23 Ⓐ Ⓑ Ⓒ Ⓓ	33 Ⓐ Ⓑ Ⓒ Ⓓ	43 Ⓐ Ⓑ Ⓒ Ⓓ
5 Ⓐ Ⓑ Ⓒ Ⓓ Ⓔ	14 Ⓕ Ⓖ Ⓗ Ⓙ	24 Ⓕ Ⓖ Ⓗ Ⓙ	34 Ⓕ Ⓖ Ⓗ Ⓙ	44 Ⓕ Ⓖ Ⓗ Ⓙ
6 Ⓕ Ⓖ Ⓗ Ⓙ Ⓚ	15 Ⓐ Ⓑ Ⓒ Ⓓ	25 Ⓐ Ⓑ Ⓒ Ⓓ	35 Ⓐ Ⓑ Ⓒ Ⓓ	45 Ⓐ Ⓑ Ⓒ Ⓓ
7 Ⓐ Ⓑ Ⓒ Ⓓ Ⓔ	16 Ⓕ Ⓖ Ⓗ Ⓙ	26 Ⓕ Ⓖ Ⓗ Ⓙ	36 Ⓕ Ⓖ Ⓗ Ⓙ	46 Ⓕ Ⓖ Ⓗ Ⓙ
8 Ⓕ Ⓖ Ⓗ Ⓙ Ⓚ	17 Ⓐ Ⓑ Ⓒ Ⓓ	27 Ⓐ Ⓑ Ⓒ Ⓓ	37 Ⓐ Ⓑ Ⓒ Ⓓ	47 Ⓐ Ⓑ Ⓒ Ⓓ
A Ⓐ Ⓑ Ⓒ Ⓓ	18 Ⓕ Ⓖ Ⓗ Ⓙ	28 Ⓕ Ⓖ Ⓗ Ⓙ	38 Ⓕ Ⓖ Ⓗ Ⓙ	48 Ⓕ Ⓖ Ⓗ Ⓙ
9 Ⓐ Ⓑ Ⓒ Ⓓ	19 Ⓐ Ⓑ Ⓒ Ⓓ	29 Ⓐ Ⓑ Ⓒ Ⓓ	39 Ⓐ Ⓑ Ⓒ Ⓓ	

0:40

Time Limit:
approx. 40 minutes

Name _____

Reading

SAMPLE A

Some people complain when their dog's hair gets all over the house. Others welcome the problem by spinning the hair into yarn and knitting with it. In some cities, you can even find craftspeople who will knit you a sweater from your dog's hair.

This passage is mostly about

A how to clean up dog hair.

B how people love their pets.

C an unusual way to use dog hair.

D why people knit sweaters.

Directions: People are sometimes surprised when they discover talents they never knew they had. Leslie is both a painter and an athlete. Read the story about how she got started painting, then do numbers 1–5.

Accidental Artist

It all started by accident. I was in a summer day camp when I was about ten. I loved sports and was disappointed when it rained. One rainy day my counselor took us to the art room. I grabbed a pencil and some paper and drew a soccer ball. It was kind of fun, so I added some grass around the ball and a pair of shoes. When it was finished, everybody—including me—was amazed at how good it was.

From then on, I still played lots of sports, but I always found time to draw and paint. When I got older and was on the high school soccer and basketball teams, I took my sketch pad with me. In the bus on the way home, I drew things that happened during the games.

When I went to college, everyone was surprised when I chose art as my major. I even got a scholarship, which really helped my parents out. I played soccer, of course, but art was the chief reason I went to college. I knew that when I finished school, I wanted to be an artist.

GO

1 This story is mostly about

    A soccer, basketball, and art.

    B a girl growing up.

    C summer camp and college.

    D how a girl became an artist.

2 At first, Leslie was most interested in

    F camp.   **H** drawing.

    G sports.   **J** studying.

3 How did Leslie feel after she completed her first drawing?

    A amazed

    B amused

    C disappointed

    D relaxed

4 Leslie's scholarship "really helped her parents out." What does this mean?

    F They wanted to be artists.

    G They wanted Leslie to be a soccer player.

    H It saved them money.

    J It surprised them.

5 The story says that Leslie was disappointed at camp when it rained. A word that means the opposite of *disappointed* is

    A saddened.

    B pleased.

    C relieved.

    D entertained.

Directions: Leslie's brother, Lee, wrote this about her. For numbers 6 and 7, find the words that best complete the paragraph.

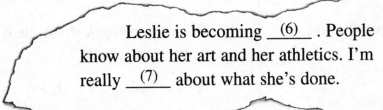

Leslie is becoming __(6)__ . People know about her art and her athletics. I'm really __(7)__ about what she's done.

6 F famous

    G released

    H exhausted

    J fragile

7 A confused

    B rejected

    C lessened

    D proud

GO

Name _____

Directions: Read the passage. Then answer questions 8–21.

Snakes

How much do you know about snakes? Read these snake facts and find out.

- A snake skeleton has **numerous** ribs. A large snake may have as many as 400 pairs!
- Most snakes have **poor** eyesight. They **track** other animals by sensing their body heat.
- Snakes can't blink! They sleep with their eyes open.
- Although all snakes have teeth, very few of them—only the **venomous** ones—have fangs.
- Many snakes are very **docile** and unlikely to bite people.
- Pet snakes recognize their owners by smell. They flick their tongues in the air to **detect** smells.
- Snakes have special ways of hearing. Sound vibrations from the earth pass through their bellies to **receptors** in their spines. **Airborne** sounds pass through snakes' lungs to receptors in their skin.

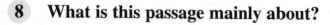

8 **What is this passage mainly about?**

   F keeping snakes as pets

   G snakes' body parts

   H venomous snakes

   J snakes' eyesight

9 **In this passage, *poor* means the opposite of**

   A rich.

   B good.

   C happy.

   D broke.

10 ***Numerous* means about the same as**

   F number.

   G many.

   H few.

   J special.

11 **What does *track* mean as it is used in this passage?**

   A the rails on which a train moves

   B a sport that includes running, jumping, and throwing

   C to follow the footprints of

   D to find and follow

GO

Test Prep

Name _____

12 **Which word is a synonym for *venomous*?**

F   vicious   H   sharp

G   poisonous   J   huge

13 **Which word means the opposite of *docile*?**

A   vicious   C   shy

B   gentle   D   active

14 **Which word means the same as *detect*?**

F   enjoy   H   arrest

G   find   J   hide

15 **A *receptor* _____ something.**

A   throws   C   takes in

B   gives   D   sees

16 **Airborne sounds are**

F   carried through the air.

G   carried through the earth.

H   always made by wind.

J   louder than other sounds.

Directions: For numbers 17–21, decide whether each statement is true or false.

17 **A large snake may have 800 pairs of ribs.**

A   true   B   false

18 **Most snakes have very good eyesight.**

A   true   B   false

19 **Everyone is a little afraid of snakes.**

A   true   B   false

20 **Only a few kinds of snakes are venomous.**

A   true   B   false

21 **Snakes detect sound in their spines and skin.**

A   true   B   false

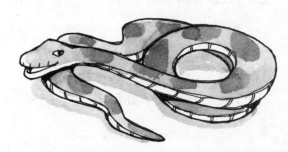

GO

Name _____

Directions: Read the following passage. Then answer questions 22–27.

HELPING THE MOUNTAIN GORILLA

Mountain gorillas live in the rainforests in Rwanda, Uganda, and the Democratic Republic of the Congo. These large, beautiful animals are becoming very rare. They have lost much of their **habitat** as people move in and take over gorillas' lands. Although there are strict laws protecting gorillas, **poachers** continue to hunt them.

Scientists observe gorillas to learn about their habits and needs. Then scientists write about their findings in magazines. Concerned readers sometimes contribute money to help safeguard the mountain gorillas.

Many other people are working hard to protect the mountain gorillas. Park rangers patrol the rainforest and arrest poachers. Tourists bring much-needed money into the area, encouraging local residents to protect the gorillas, too.

22 **What is this passage mainly about?**

A mountain gorillas' family relationships

B scientists who study mountain gorillas

C ways that gorillas are threatened and helped

D poachers and wars that threaten gorillas' survival

23 **Which words help you figure out the meaning of *habitat*?**

F "large, beautiful animals"

G "gorillas' lands"

H "the human population"

J "recent civil wars"

24 **In this passage, *poacher* means**

A park ranger.

B mountain gorilla.

C unlawful hunter.

D scientist.

25 **The writer of the passage thinks that tourism**

F is very harmful to mountain gorillas.

G is one cause of civil wars in Africa.

H can be helpful to mountain gorillas.

J is one cause of overpopulation in Africa.

GO

Name _____

Directions: For numbers 26 and 27, decide whether each statement is true or false.

26 **Mountain gorillas live in African deserts.**

    A true   **B** false

27 **People who live near the mountain gorillas have little need for money.**

    A true   **B** false

Directions: For numbers 28–31, choose the correct answer to each question.

28 **Apple is to orange as lettuce is to _____ .**

    A grapefruit   **C** apple

    B vegetable   **D** spinach

29 **Happy is to sad as beautiful is to _____ .**

    F ugly   **H** pretty

    G unhappy   **J** angry

30 **Car is to driver as train is to _____ .**

    A passenger   **C** conductor

    B headmaster   **D** inspector

31 **Jupiter is to planet as United States is to _____ .**

    F Washington, D. C.

    G state

    H nation

    J North America

Directions: Match words with the same meanings.

32	ruin	**A**	annoy
33	aid	**B**	attempt
34	try	**C**	help
35	irritate	**D**	destroy

Directions: Match words with opposite meanings.

36	funny	**F**	boring
37	exciting	**G**	nice
38	mature	**H**	serious
39	mean	**J**	childish

STOP

0:35
Time Limit:
approx. 35 minutes

Name _____

Language Arts

Directions: For Sample A and numbers 1 and 2, read the sentences. Choose the word that correctly completes both sentences.

> **SAMPLE A** **Do you feel _____ ?**
> **We get our water from a _____ .**
>
> **A** well   **B** good   **C** pipe   **D** sick

1 It's not safe to _____ a boat.
This _____ is too heavy to move.

  A sink   **C** push

  B stone   **D** rock

2 The photography _____ meets today.
The cave man carried a _____ .

  F group   **H** spear

  G club   **J** class

Directions: For numbers 3 and 4, read the paragraph. For each numbered blank, choose the word that best completes the paragraph.

Roller Blading

In-line skating, also known as rollerblading, might be the fastest growing __(3)__ in America. Each day, millions of people step into their skates and take off for miles of exercise and enjoyment. Typical __(4)__ follow roads, sidewalks, or bikepaths, but "extreme skaters" build half-pipes of plywood or seek expert terrain like steps or steep hills. This sport is relatively new, but it is already enjoyed by people young and old.

3 **A** thing

  B people

  C town

  D sport

4 **F** skaters

  G vehicles

  H hikers

  J results

GO

Name _____

Directions: For number 5, decide which punctuation mark, if any, is needed in the sentence.

5 **"Your brother just called," said Kyle.**

.	,	!	None
A	**B**	**C**	**D**

Directions: For numbers 6 and 7, choose the answer that is written correctly and shows the correct capitalization and punctuation.

6 **F** Mrs. shields writes about sports for our local newspaper.

   G Did Dr. Robinson call yet?

   H Please give this to miss Young.

   J This is Mr McCoy's bicycle.

7 **A** I cant see the game from here.

   B Kim wasn't able to play this week.

   C Dont' worry if you forgot.

   D The coach would'nt let us in.

Directions: For numbers 8 and 9, look at the underlined part of each sentence. Choose the answer that shows the best capitalization and punctuation for that part.

(8) We moved into our new house on June 5, 2001.

(9) The garage bathroom, and kitchen still weren't finished.

8 **F** June 5 2001

   G June, 5 2001

   H june 5 2001

   J Correct as it is

9 **A** garage, bathroom, and

   B garage bathroom, and,

   C garage, bathroom. And

   D Correct as it is

GO

Name _____

Directions: For numbers 10–13, choose the word that is spelled correctly and best completes the sentence.

10   **This _____ leads to the gym.**

   F   stareway

   G   stareweigh

   H   stairweigh

   J   stairway

11   **Hand me the _____ , please.**

   A   chalk

   B   chaulk

   C   chawlk

   D   challk

12   **We went on a _____ walk.**

   F   nachur

   G   nature

   H   nayture

   J   nachure

13   **Please _____ your work.**

   A   revew

   B   reeview

   C   review

   D   revyoo

Directions: For numbers 14–17, read each phrase. Find the underlined word that is <u>not</u> spelled correctly. If all the underlined words are spelled correctly, mark "All correct."

14   **F**   <u>shallow</u> water

   G   confusing <u>signal</u>

   H   find <u>something</u>

   J   <u>sparkle</u> brightly

   K   All correct

15   **A**   no <u>trouble</u>

   B   <u>unusual</u> bird

   C   play the <u>violin</u>

   D   cat's <u>whisker</u>

   E   All correct

16   **F**   white <u>geese</u>

   G   <u>lively</u> conversation

   H   <u>relaxing</u> music

   J   local <u>libary</u>

   K   All correct

17   **A**   good <u>condition</u>

   B   book <u>shelvs</u>

   C   <u>through</u> the door

   D   <u>eagerly</u> waiting

   E   All correct

GO

Name _____

Directions: For numbers 18-25, find the answer that shows the correct capitalization and punctuation.

18 521 north Main st

   F 521 North Main st

   G 521 North Main St

   H 521 North Main St.

   J Correct as is

19 West Hills, PA 11123

   A West hills, Pa 11123

   B West Hills PA 11123

   C West Hills, pa 11123

   D Correct as is

20 aug 12 2001

   F AUG 12, 2001

   G Aug. 12, 2001

   H Aug. 12 2001

   J Correct as is

21 Mrs Ann c James

   A Mrs. Ann c. James

   B Mrs. Ann C James

   C Mrs. Ann C. James

   D Correct as is

22 432 East oak Ave

   F 432 East Oak Ave

   G 432 East Oak Ave.

   H 432 east Oak Ave.

   J Correct as is

23 Newton valley oh 42111

   A Newton Valley, OH 42111

   B Newton Valley OH 42111

   C Newton Valley, oh 42111

   D Correct as is

24 dear mrs. James

   F Dear mrs. James,

   G Dear Mrs. James—

   H Dear Mrs. James,

   J Correct as is

25 thank you for the cool camera

   A Thank you, for the cool camera

   B thank you for the cool camera.

   C Thank you for the cool camera.

   D Correct as is

GO

Name _____

Directions: For numbers 26-33, find the sentence that is correctly written.

26
F Those muffins was delicious!

G Those blueberries is so sweet and juicy.

H We done picked them yesterday afternoon.

J Please have another muffin.

27
A We are awful glad you made it.

B We've been waiting anxiously.

C The roads are real bad.

D It's been snowing something heavy for hours.

28
F Ray and I raked the leaves into a huge pile.

G My friend Ann helped him and I.

H Her and I jumped onto the leaf pile

J Ray took a great picture of me and her.

29
A Of all the days for the bus to be late.

B We had to wait in the pouring rain.

C Even though I had an umbrella.

D Absolutely soaked by the time it came.

30
F Last night at 7 o'clock in the school auditorium.

G The third annual school talent show.

H Our class put on the funniest skit of the show.

J Heard my parents laughing and applauding.

31
A I was late because the bus broke down.

B I was late even though the bus broked down.

C I was late the bus broke down.

D I was late because the bus is broke.

32
F Dan ate a sandwich and a apple.

G Jake has a cup of soup and a salad.

H May I please have a extra cookie?

J I'd like an ham and cheese omelet?

33
A Come and see this spider.

B Watched curiously as it spun.

C Here an unsuspecting fly.

D How patiently the spider?

GO

Name _____

Directions: For numbers 34–43, find the word that completes the sentence and is spelled correctly.

34 That is the _____ story I've ever read.

   F funniest   **H** funnyst

   G funnyest   **J** funnest

35 I grew three _____ this year.

   A inchs   **C** inchys

   B inchies   **D** inches

36 We planted _____ along the fence.

   F daisyes   **H** daisys

   G daisies   **J** daises

37 My brother _____ the coolest gift.

   A recieved   **C** received

   B receeved   **D** receaved

38 I _____ at the store after school.

   F stopt   **H** stoppt

   G stoped   **J** stopped

39 He is my best _____ .

   A frind   **C** friend

   B frend   **D** freind

40 Miss Lambert was _____ about the litter on her lawn.

   F fuious   **H** furius

   G furious   **J** fiurius

41 I can't _____ it!

   A belive   **C** beleive

   B believe   **D** beleve

42 Her cousin is the most _____ person I've ever met.

   F polight

   G pollite

   H pollight

   J polite

43 The garage needed a _____ cleaning.

   A thoroh

   B thurow

   C thourough

   D thorough

GO

Name _____ Test Prep

Directions: Find the punctuation mark that is missing from each sentence.

44 **Jody please don't forget to feed the cat.**

   '   !   ,   Correct as is

  F   **G**   **H**   **J**

45 **Max said hed help me rake the leaves.**

  "   '   ,   Correct as is

  A   **B**   **C**   **D**

46 **"Why aren't you coming with us" asked Julie.**

  .   ,   ?   Correct as is

  F   **G**   **H**   **J**

47 **No, we're not going to the mall today.**

  '   ,   "   Correct as is

  A   **B**   **C**   **D**

48 **I ate the whole box I had such a stomach ache!**

  ,   !   ;   Correct as is

  F   **G**   **H**   **J**

Directions: For numbers 49–51, find the answer with the correct capitalization of the underlined words.

49 **The last thing I meant to do was annoy the Andersons on arbor day.**

  A annoy the andersons on arbor day

  B Annoy The Andersons on arbor day

  C annoy the Andersons on Arbor Day

  D Correct as is

50 **The neighbors got back from a long trip to the south of china.**

  F south of China

  G South of china

  H South Of China

  J Correct as is

51 **Somehow, the shoe landed on Felipe sanchez's lawn.**

  A felipe sanchez's lawn

  B Felipe Sanchez's lawn

  C Felipe Sanchez's Lawn

  D Correct as is

STOP

0:30

Time Limit:
approx. 30 minutes

Name _____

Directions: Read the paragraph that tells about one student's great experience. Then think about all the good experiences you have ever had. Write one or two sentences to answer each question below.

> My violin competition was one of the best experiences I've ever had. I met people from all over the city. I learned to feel comfortable in front of an audience. I felt good about playing for so many people. When everyone clapped, I felt very proud.

Think about all your good experiences. Which one was the best?

_____

_____

_____

Why was this experience so good?

_____

_____

_____

How did the experience make you feel?

_____

_____

_____

GO

Name _____

Directions: Read the paragraph below about how to plant a seed. Then think of something you know how to do. Write a paragraph that explains how to do it. Use words such as *first*, *next*, *then*, *finally*, *last*.

I found out how to plant a seed and make it grow. First, I found a spot where the plant would get the right amount of sunshine. Next, I dug a hole, put the seed into the soil, and then covered the seed with soil. Then I watered the seed. After a couple weeks it began to grow into a beautiful plant.

_____

_____

_____

_____

_____

_____

_____

_____

_____

_____

_____

_____

_____

_____

STOP

0:45

Time Limit:
approx. 45 minutes

Name _____

Mathematics

1

282
422
+ 116

A 810

B 710

C 830

D 819

E None of these

2

$0.6 - 0.6 =$

F 0

G 0.8

H 0.04

J 1

K None of these

3

$2 \times 5 \times 9 =$

A 16

B 47

C 19

D 91

E None of these

4

$4\frac{6}{11}$
$+ 3\frac{2}{11}$

F 8

G $1\frac{4}{11}$

H $7\frac{8}{11}$

J $1\frac{8}{11}$

K None of these

5

37
× 8

A 296

B 255

C 45

D 166

E None of these

6

$88 \div 8 =$

F 8

G 0

H 1

J 11

K None of these

7

2.5
− 1.5

A 1.5

B 3.0

C 3.5

D 5

E None of these

8

$2\frac{1}{5} + 1\frac{3}{5} =$

F 4

G $1\frac{2}{5}$

H $3\frac{4}{5}$

J $3\frac{2}{5}$

K None of these

GO

Name _____

SAMPLE A Hillary spent between $11 and $12. Which two items did she buy?

A leash and food   **C** collar and food

B collar and leash   **D** collar and bowl

$3.89

$6.20

$9.75

$4.95

COLLECTING BASEBALL CARDS

Directions: The binders below show four students' baseball card collections. Look at the picture. Then do numbers 9 and 10.

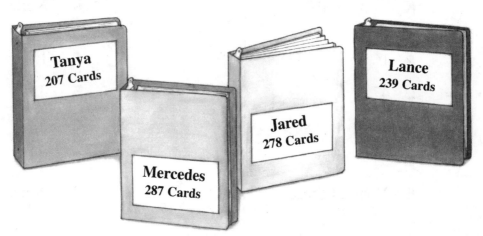

Tanya
207 Cards

Mercedes
287 Cards

Jared
278 Cards

Lance
239 Cards

9 The plastic inserts in the binders hold 9 cards each. Which student has a notebook in which every inserted page is full?

   A Tanya

   B Mercedes

   C Jared

   D Lance

10 Which of these shows the baseball card collections arranged from fewest cards to most?

   F Tanya, Lance, Mercedes, Jared

   G Tanya, Lance, Jared, Mercedes

   H Lance, Tanya, Mercedes, Jared

   J Mercedes, Jared, Lance, Tanya

GO

Name _____

Rainy Day Game

Directions: The picture shows spinners made by four children who used them in a game. Look at the spinners. Then do numbers 11 and 12.

11 **Whose spinner will land on a square more than half the time?**

    A Marci's

    B Eric's

    C Jeffrey's

    D Lauren's

12 **Whose spinner has the best chance of landing on a triangle?**

    F Marci's

    G Eric's

    H Jeffrey's

    J Lauren's

GO

Name _____

13 Jodi bought cans of tennis balls that cost $2.50 per can. What else do you need to know to find out how much money Jodi spent in all?

   A whether she played singles or doubles

   B how many cans of tennis balls she bought

   C whether she won her tennis match

   D how many cans of tennis balls the store had in stock

14 The computer screen shows some of the top scores earned on a computer game. Ricky earned the top score at level 10. Which was most likely his score?

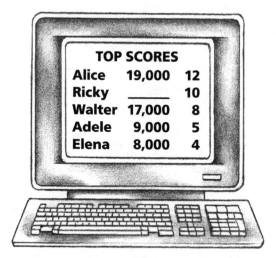

TOP SCORES		
Alice	19,000	12
Ricky	_____	10
Walter	17,000	8
Adele	9,000	5
Elena	8,000	4

   F 17,000

   G 18,000

   H 20,000

   J 21,000

15 To win at this board game, you need to cover 16 spaces with chips you earn. How many more chips does Marla need to earn so that she can cover $\frac{3}{4}$ of her spaces?

   A 1

   B 2

   C 3

   D 4

GO

Test Prep

Name _____

16 Lillian rode her bicycle to the supermarket for her mother. Here is the change she was given when she bought one of the items on the table with a five-dollar bill. Which item did she buy?

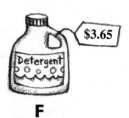   

$3.65 $4.55 $3.50 $4.79

    F   **G**   **H**   **J**

17 Yoshi used this clue to find the secret number to open the briefcase. What is the secret number?

   A 12

   B 10

   C 8

   D 6

If you double the secret number and then add 4, the answer is 20.

18 Which of these figures is $\frac{4}{7}$ shaded?

    F   **G**   **H**   **J**

GO

Name _____

Directions: Choose the answer that correctly solves each problem.

19

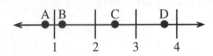

What point represents $\frac{3}{4}$?

A A   **B** B   **C** C   **D** D

20 **What is the next number in this pattern?**

1 2 4 8 16 32 64....

F 80 **G** 81 **H** 84 **J** 128

21 **Which figure is symmetric?**

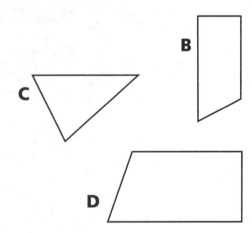

22 **How many sides does a rectangle have?**

F 0 **G** 2 **H** 3 **J** 4

23 **Which unit would be best for measuring the length of a new pencil?**

A feet

B meters

C inches

D liters

CENTER CINEMAS
MOVIE TICKET SALES

MONDAY
TUESDAY
WEDNESDAY
THURSDAY
FRIDAY

KEY: 10 TICKETS =

24 **How many more tickets were sold on Friday than on Tuesday?**

F 45 **G** 55 **H** 75 **J** 295

25 **Which number has an 8 in the thousands place?**

A 81,428

B 78,643

C 42,638

D 29,821

GO

26 **What is the perimeter of the rectangle?**

   F   22 meters

   G 18 meters

   H 11 meters

   J   3 meters

4 meters

7 meters

27 **How many sides does a circle have?**

   A 12   **B** 2   **C** 1   **D** 0

28 **What is the temperature on the thermometer?**

   F 87 °F

   G 82 °F

   H 80 °F

   J   78 °F

29 **What is the least favorite pet in Ms. Sheely's class?**

   A dog

   B cat

   C gerbil

   D fish

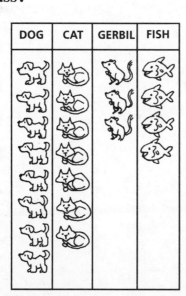

30 **What fraction does the shaded portion of the picture represent?**

   F $\frac{1}{4}$

   G $\frac{1}{3}$

   H $\frac{1}{2}$

   J $1\frac{1}{4}$

31 **Which letter has a line of symmetry?**

   A J   **B** S   **C** M   **D** Q

32 **What picture shows a fraction equivalent to $\frac{3}{10}$?**

   F

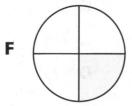

   G

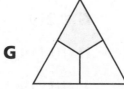

   H

   J

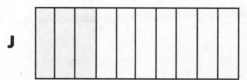

GO

Name _____

Directions: Choose the answer that correctly solves each problem.

33

$879 + 43 =$

A 1,309
B 922
C 836
D 122

34

$46 \times 82 =$

F 3,772
G 3,672
H 3,662
J 128

35

$281 - 93 =$

A 188
B 212
C 288
D 374

36

$8,941 + 1,278 =$

F 9,119
G 9,219
H 10,119
J 10,219

37

$369 \times 4 =$

A 1,476
B 1,264
C 123
D 92

38

$445 \div 6 =$

F 78 R1
G 63 R4
H 74 R3
J None of these

39

$84.62 \ \square \ 84.26$

A >
B =
C <
D None of these

40

$\frac{1}{4} + \frac{3}{4} =$

F $\frac{2}{4}$
G $\frac{1}{2}$
H 1
J 4

41

$431 + 622 + 58 =$

A 1110
B 1010
C 111
D None of these

42

$12 \times 12 =$

F 240
G 144
H 140
J 24

GO

Name _____

Directions: Choose the answer that correctly solves each problem.

43 Colleen found 16 shells on Saturday and 17 shells on Sunday. Al found 12 shells on Saturday and 22 shells on Sunday. Who found the greater number of shells altogether?

   A Al

   B Colleen

   C They each found the same number of shells.

   D Not enough information

44 Angela saved her allowance to buy a new pair of sneakers. She had $70.00. After buying the sneakers, how much money did she have left?

   F $9.25

   G $8.75

   H $7.65

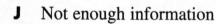

   J Not enough information

45 David has 72 baseball cards that he is sorting into three equal piles. How many cards are in each pile?

   A 216 cards

   B 24 cards

   C 20 R4 cards

   D 18 cards

46 Toby left his house for school at 7:35 a.m. He arrived to school at 7:50 a.m. How many minutes did it take Toby to get to school?

   F 15 minutes

   G 20 minutes

   H 25 minutes

   J 10 minutes

47 Rosendo and his sister combine their money to buy a new game. Rosendo has $7.48 and his sister has $8.31. How much money do they have in all?

   A $0.83

   B $15.79

   C $16.89

   D Not enough information

48 What equation would you use to solve the following problem?

Tyrone and Lawrence have a total of 26 CDs. They each have the same number of CDs. How many CDs does Tyrone have?

   F $26 \times 2 =$

   G $26 + 2 =$

   H $26 - 2 =$

   J $26 \div 2 =$

STOP

Grade 4 Answer Key

Page 16
A. D
B. F

Page 18
1. B
2. H
3. A

Page 19
4. J
5. C
6. F

Page 20
7. D
8. F
9. C

Page 22
10. G
11. A
12. J
13. A

Page 23
14. J
15. C
16. F
17. B

Page 24
18. J
19. C
20. F
21. B

Page 25
C. C

Page 26

Page 27
22. D
23. J

24. A
25. H
26. C
27. J

Page 28
D. B
28. C
29. J

Page 29
30. A
31. J

Page 30
32. D
33. H
34. B

Page 31
A. D
1. B
2. J
B. A
3. C
4. F

Page 32
5. B
6. H
7. B
8. H
9. D
10. G

Page 33

C. C
11. B
12. H
13. B
14. J

Page 34
15. C
16. F
17. A
18. H
19. D
20. G

Page 35
D. D
21. D
22. F
E. E
23. A
24. J

Pages 36 and 37
Answers will vary.

Grade 4 Answer Key

Page 38
F. A
25. A
26. H
G. B
27. C
28. H

Page 39
29. D
30. F
31. D
32. J
33. A
34. H
35. B

Page 40
36. F
37. C
38. J
39. D
40. F
41. E
42. H
43. D

Page 41
Answers
will vary.

Page 42
A. B
B. K
1. D
2. F
3. B
4. G

Page 43
C. C

Page 44
5. C
6. G

Page 45
7. D
8. F
9. C

Page 46
10. J
11. A
12. G

Page 47
13. C
14. G
15. C

Page 48
16. J
17. A
18. K
19. B
20. H
21. D
22. F
23. C

Page 49
D. D
24. C
25. H

Page 50
26. D
27. H
28. C

Page 51
29. H
30. C
31. F

Page 54
A. C

Page 55
1. D
2. G
3. A
4. H
5. B
6. F
7. D

Page 56
8. G
9. B
10. G
11. D

Page 57
12. G
13. A
14. G
15. C
16. F
17. B
18. B
19. B
20. A
21. A

Page 58
22. C
23. G
24. C
25. H

Page 59
26. B
27. B
28. D
29. F
30. C
31. H
32. D
33. C
34. B
35. A
36. H
37. F
38. J
39. G

Page 60
A. A
1. D
2. G
3. D
4. F

Page 61
5. D
6. G
7. B
8. J
9. A

Grade 4 Answer Key

Page 62
10. J
11. A
12. G
13. C
14. G
15. E
16. J
17. B

Page 63
18. H
19. D
20. G
21. C
22. G
23. A
24. H
25. C

Page 64
26. J
27. B
28. F
29. B
30. H
31. A
32. G
33. A

Page 65
34. F
35. D
36. G
37. C
38. J
39. C
40. G
41. B
42. J
43. D

Page 66
44. H
45. B
46. H
47. D
48. H
49. C
50. F
51. B

Page 69
1. E
2. F
3. E
4. H
5. A
6. J
7. E
8. H

Page 70
A. D
9. A
10. G

Page 71
11. B
12. J

Page 72
13. B
14. G
15. C

Page 73
16. F
17. C
18. J

Page 74
19. A
20. J
21. A
22. J
23. C
24. G
25. B

Page 75
26. F
27. D
28. G
29. C
30. F
31. C
32. J

Page 76
33. B
34. F
35. A
36. J
37. A
38. J
39. A
40. H
41. D
42. G

Page 77
43. A
44. H
45. B
46. F
47. B
48. J